Partners in the Sea

TEXT BY MARY JO RHODES AND DAVID HALL
PHOTOGRAPHS BY DAVID HALL

Undersea Encounters

Children's Press®
A Division of Scholastic Inc.
New York   Toronto   London   Auckland   Sydney
Mexico City   New Delhi   Hong Kong
Danbury, Connecticut

Library of Congress Cataloging-in-Publication Data

Rhodes, Mary Jo, 1957-
    Partners in the sea / Text by Mary Jo Rhodes and David Hall; Photographs by David Hall.
        p. cm. — (Undersea encounters)
    Includes bibliographical references and index.
    ISBN 0-516-24397-7 (lib. bdg.) 0-516-25492-8 (pbk.)
    1. Marine animals—Behavior—Juvenile literature. 2. Symbiosis—Juvenile literature.
I. Hall, David, 1943 Oct. 2– II. Title. III. Series.
    QL122.2.R49 2005
    591.77—dc22
                                            2005003684

To my younger diving "partners" Jessica, Jamie, Maya, Aron, Noah, Jenny, Dan, and Becky,
whose enthusiasm helped to inspire this book.
—D.H.

To my "symbiotic partner" in the Undersea Encounters series, David Hall, for his first-hand
knowledge of and deep appreciation for all undersea creatures.
—M.J.R.

The authors would also like to acknowledge our publishing partners:
Rosemary Stimola, for helping us turn an idea into reality;
and Meredith DeSousa, for her patience, support, and great ideas.

Unless otherwise indicated, all underwater photographs in this book were made in British Columbia or California.

All photographs © 2005 by David Hall except: Seapics.com/David B. Fleetham: 35.

Small shrimps and crabs can "catch a ride" on a jellyfish.
pg. **31**

Armed with sea anemones for protection, this boxer crab doesn't pull any punches!
pg. **25**

Partners in the Sea

Featherstars are home sweet home for small fish.
pg. **28**

A rainbow runner swims with a silvertip shark, hoping to share scraps from the shark's next meal.

chapter 1

Undersea Partnerships

Working with a friend is often better than working alone. You may be able to work faster and better than if you did not have help. Many people also have animal partners, such as cats, dogs, and horses. We feed and protect our partners. In turn, they help us in different ways.

Animals that live in the sea also form partnerships. These relationships help them to survive. Scientists call these partnerships **symbiosis** (SIM-bee-o-sis), which means "living together." There are many kinds of symbiotic relationships in the ocean.

Good for Both Partners

Some relationships are helpful to both partners. For example, a small fish called a goby lives with a blind shrimp. The shrimp is good at digging with its powerful claws. It digs a hole in which both partners can live.

The goby cannot dig, but it has good eyesight. While the shrimp is digging, the goby watches out for enemies. The shrimp keeps one antenna on the goby's tail. At the first sign of danger, the goby warns the shrimp with a flick of its tail. Both partners dash into the burrow for safety.

This teamwork is good for both partners. The blind shrimp is warned of approaching danger. In return, the goby has a safe place to live. This kind of symbiosis is called **mutualism** (MEW-chew-ul-izm).

This fish and shrimp are partners.
They live together in a burrow
that is made by the shrimp.

Good for One Partner

Sometimes, one partner benefits and the other is
not affected. For example, a small animal may
gain protection by living with a larger animal.
The large partner is called a **host**.

A tiny fish called a blenny finds protection in a hole surrounded by green coral animals.

A small fish called a blenny lives in the middle of a large coral colony. There, the fish is safe from **predators** (PRED-uh-tors). It is also in a good location for finding food.

The coral animals do not benefit from the blenny's presence, but the blenny causes them no harm. This relationship is good for one partner and does not hurt the other. Scientists call this a **commensal** (kuh-MEN-sul) relationship.

Bad for One Partner

Sometimes a relationship benefits one partner while harming the other. A **parasite** (PAR-uh-site) is a small animal that feeds on a larger host. Most **species** (SPEE-sees) of fish sometimes have parasites. A parasite can make its host very sick or even kill it.

This fish has been made sick by a parasite, which has laid eggs inside the fish's head.

One kind of parasite is a copepod (CO-puh-pod). Copepods attach themselves to the outside of a fish and suck the fish's blood. Some kinds of parasites burrow into the host's body to lay their eggs.

Sea Partners Fact

Corals are small animals that usually grow in large groups, or "colonies." Over time, they can create large underwater structures called **coral reefs**. More than one-quarter of all animals living on coral reefs are involved in helpful partnerships.

These brown barrel sponges, yellow tube sponges, and pink vase sponges are growing in shallow water.

chapter 2

Living with Sponges

Sponges are among the best partners in the ocean. The grooves and openings in a sponge give smaller animals places to hide. The water flowing through the sponge brings food to its partners.

Sponges are a kind of **invertebrate** (in-VER-tuh-brate) animal. They have no brains, stomachs, nerves, or muscles. Because they do not move at all, they seem more like plants than animals.

Sponges come in many different shapes and colors. On the outside, a sponge has openings for seawater to flow through its body. On the inside, water travels through net-like structures. These "nets" trap tiny floating animals and plants for the sponge to eat. This method of catching food is called **filter feeding**.

Sponge Hosts

One type of sponge is the giant brown or tan barrel sponge. These sponges may grow large enough for a person to climb inside. They are hosts for many kinds of fish and other animals.

Tiny pink fairy crabs live in cracks and crevices on the surface of a barrel sponge.

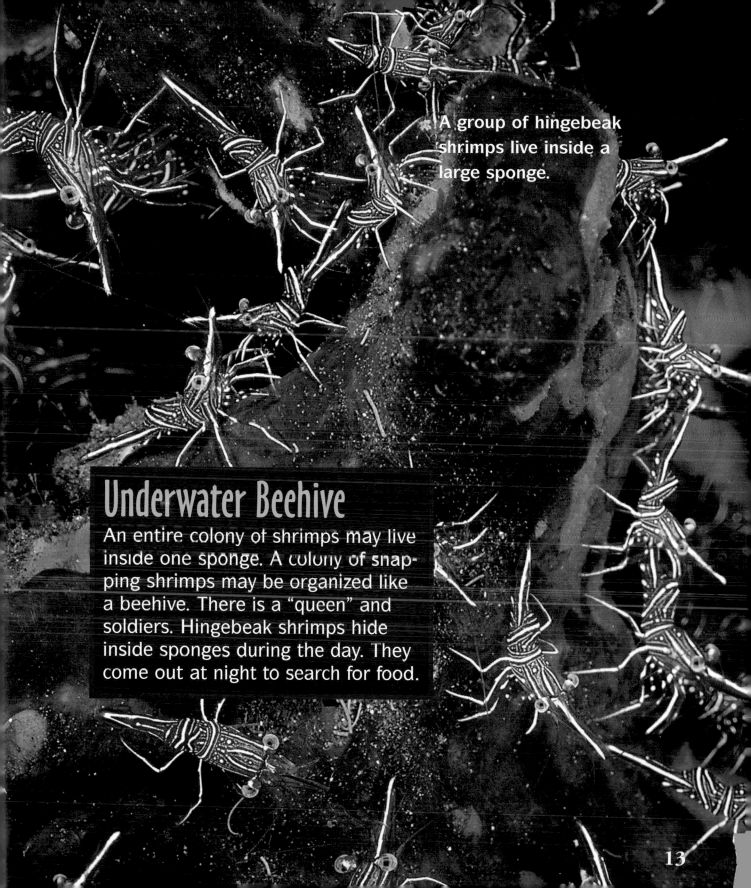

A group of hingebeak shrimps live inside a large sponge.

Underwater Beehive

An entire colony of shrimps may live inside one sponge. A colony of snapping shrimps may be organized like a beehive. There is a "queen" and soldiers. Hingebeak shrimps hide inside sponges during the day. They come out at night to search for food.

Some sponges are shaped like a vase. The azure vase sponge is one of the most beautiful. Like barrel sponges, vase sponges host a wide variety of small animals.

Other sponges are long and hollow, like a pipe. Sea star relatives called brittle stars and other small animals hide inside these sponges during the day. At night, they come out to find food.

A brittle star climbs out ▶ onto the surface of an azure vase sponge at night. It hides inside the sponge during the day.

◀ This moray eel is hunting for small animals that may be living inside a yellow tube sponge.

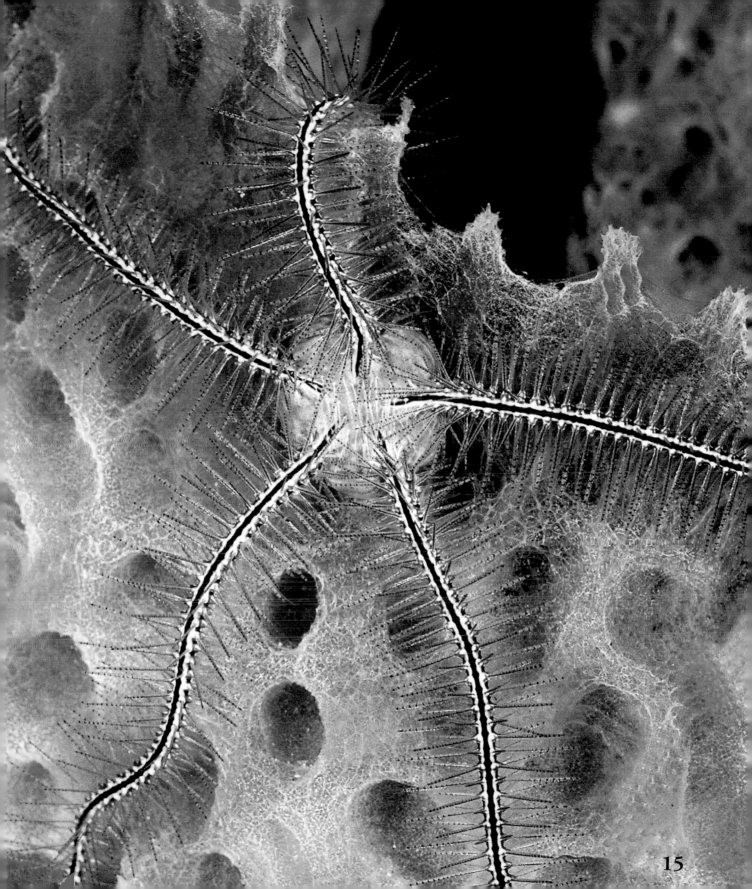

15

Sponge Clothing

Sponge Crab

The sponge crab has a special pair of legs for holding a sponge on its back. It uses its claws to tear off a piece of sponge that is just the right size. Sponge crabs look as if they are wearing sponge hats!

Decorator Crab

Some crabs attach sponges to their shells. Crabs that attach living things to themselves are called decorator crabs. The "sponge clothing" helps to disguise the crab.

Teardrop Crab

When it is young, the teardrop crab attaches a piece of red sponge to its shell. Eventually the sponge grows. It spreads to cover the entire crab. This red covering disguises the crab. It also gives it a bad taste that predators do not like.

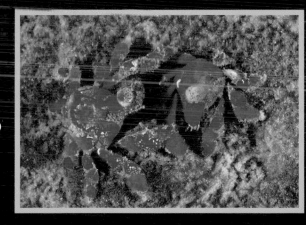

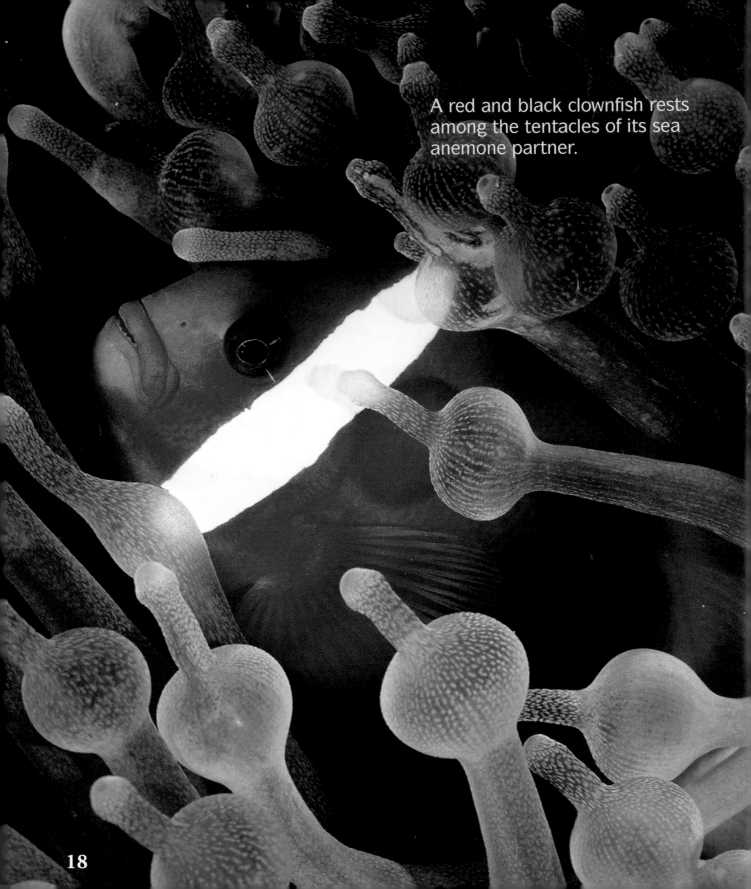

A red and black clownfish rests among the tentacles of its sea anemone partner.

chapter 3

Clownfish and Sea Anemones

A small fish swims close and touches what looks like a pretty undersea flower. Suddenly, tiny poisonous darts shoot out from the flower and stun the fish. The fish is then pulled into the mouth of the "flower" and eaten.

Sea anemones (uh-NEM-uh-nees) look like flowers, but they are really animal predators. They have mouths surrounded by stinging tentacles (TENT-uh-culs). But there are some

This large sea anemone hosts a
family of two-bar clownfish.

small fish, like the clownfish, that live safely
among those deadly tentacles.

Clownfish

There are more than two dozen kinds of clownfish. An adult clownfish is similar in size to a
goldfish. Its name comes from the bright colors

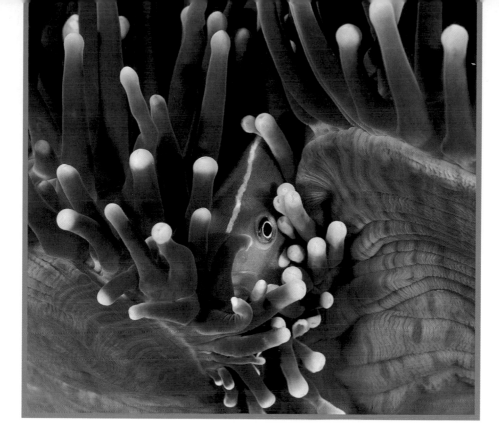

A skunk clownfish sleeps among the tentacles of its sea anemone partner.

it wears, like the costume of a circus clown. Most clownfish are colored yellow, orange, or red. Most also have one or more white stripes.

Sea Partners Fact

Scientists believe that the coating of a clownfish protects it from being stung by the anemone. The mucus in its coating may signal the anemone not to sting its partner.

A clownfish never strays far from its sea anemone host. The anemone's stinging tentacles protect the fish but do not sting it. When danger approaches, the clownfish darts into the tentacles for safety. At night, the small fish sleeps among the anemone's tentacles. It is easy to see why clownfish are sometimes also called anemonefish.

Who Benefits?

Clownfish are not very good swimmers. Without the anemone, they would soon be caught and eaten by larger fish. It is clear that the fish needs the anemone. But does the anemone also need the clownfish?

Experiments have shown that some clownfish help their anemones. They are like watchdogs, chasing other fish away. (A few fish are able to eat anemones without getting stung.) So in some cases, the relationship helps both partners.

These saddleback clownfish are ready to defend their anemone by driving off any other animals that come too close.

A Sea Anemone Home

Each sea anemone hosts one adult male and one female clownfish. Often there are several younger fish as well. When a female clownfish is ready to lay eggs, she picks a spot near the anemone. The male then fertilizes the eggs. He guards them for about a week until they hatch.

This pair of clownfish is guarding their eggs, which are placed on a rock near the base of the anemone.

After hatching, a baby clownfish drifts in the ocean. After one to two weeks, it settles down on the seafloor. It must quickly find an anemone in which to live, or it will become a meal for a larger fish.

Sea Partners Fact

What happens when a female clownfish dies? Her male partner changes sex and takes her place! Then one of the younger fish matures quickly to become the new adult male.

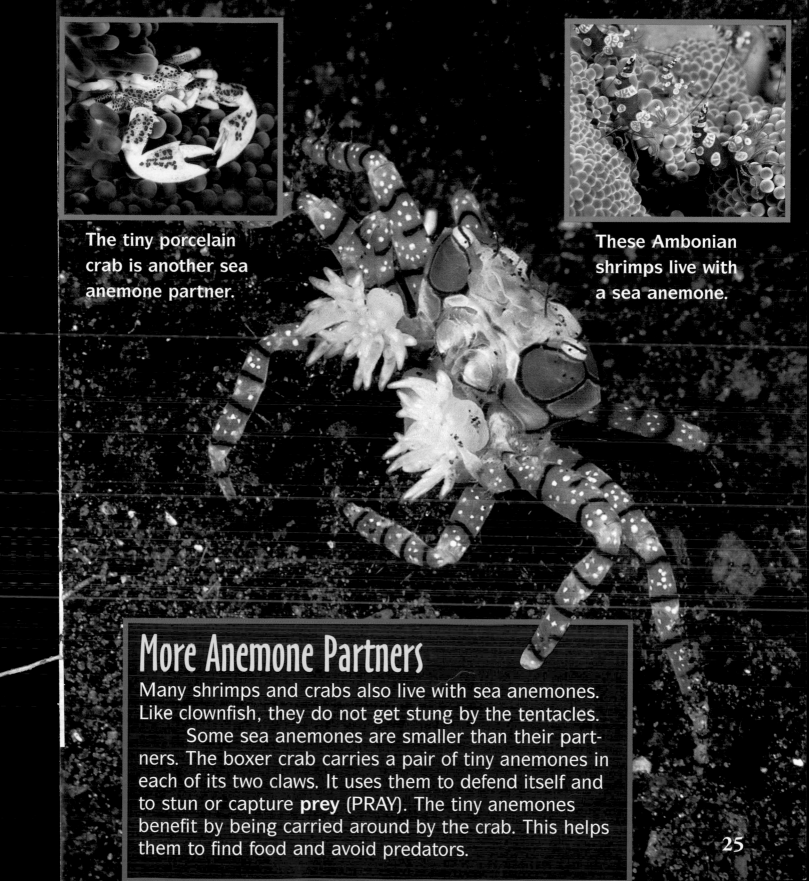

The tiny porcelain crab is another sea anemone partner.

These Ambonian shrimps live with a sea anemone.

More Anemone Partners

Many shrimps and crabs also live with sea anemones. Like clownfish, they do not get stung by the tentacles.

Some sea anemones are smaller than their partners. The boxer crab carries a pair of tiny anemones in each of its two claws. It uses them to defend itself and to stun or capture **prey** (PRAY). The tiny anemones benefit by being carried around by the crab. This helps them to find food and avoid predators.

25

A pair of Coleman's shrimps ride on the back of a sea urchin.

chapter 4

Piggyback Partners

A piggyback ride is fun for children, but for some sea animals it is a way of life. Invertebrates called **echinoderms** (ee-KI-no-derms) are especially good animal partners to ride on. *Echinoderm* means "spiny skin." Spiny-skinned partners are related to starfish. They include featherstars, sea urchins, and sea cucumbers. These animals are like the taxicabs of the undersea world.

Featherstar Partners

Featherstars are sea star relatives with long, feathery arms. They move by "walking" slowly on their arms. Like sponges, featherstars are filter feeders. They trap and eat tiny plants and animals floating in the water.

A tiny gold and white shrimp lives among the arms of featherstar.

A small fish, called a "clingfish," also lives with a featherstar host.

Shrimps and crabs live among the arms of featherstars. Small fish also cling to their bodies. For added protection, these animals are colored to blend in with their host.

Sea Urchin Partners

Sea urchins have a round shell and long, sharp spines. Small fish sometimes swim between the spines. Predators cannot reach them there.

This young fish is safe from predators while it swims among the sharp spines of a black sea urchin.

The spines covering some sea urchins can cause a painful sting. A pair of tiny Coleman's shrimps ride piggyback on these "fire urchins." The shrimps remove some of the urchin's poisonous spines to make a small home for themselves.

Sea Cucumber Partners

A sea cucumber has a fat, wormlike body. A mouth surrounded by tentacles is at one end.

An imperial shrimp rides on the back of its sea cucumber partner.

Most sea cucumbers creep along slowly on the seafloor and feed on decaying plants and animals. They often carry small partners, such as shrimps, crabs, and worms. The small pearlfish lives inside the sea cucumber's body. It is a parasite that nibbles on its host's organs.

Jellyfish Partners

Jellyfish are like swimming sea anemones. Small crabs and shrimps may use jellyfish for transportation. Small fish often live among the stinging tentacles of a jellyfish. Like clownfish, these fish gain protection from predators without being stung.

This tiny crab is going for a ride on the upside-down jellyfish.

A small cleaner fish is offering its services to a passing emperor angelfish. Cleaner fish often have a bold, striped pattern so that other fish will recognize them.

chapter 5

Undersea Doctors

When a fish gets sick, it goes to a "doctor." Fish doctors are called cleaners. They remove parasites from their patients' skin and mouths. These cleaners also remove dead or diseased skin. In this kind of partnership, the cleaner also benefits because it eats the parasites that it removes.

Cleaning Stations

Anywhere cleaners are at work is called a cleaning station. Fish visit cleaning

Fish at a cleaning station signal that they are waiting to be cleaned. Some of them float with their tails pointing down. Others spread their fins or open their mouths wide.

stations regularly to have their parasites removed. If the cleaners have a lot of "customers," a fish may have to wait in line.

While it is being cleaned, a fish seems to go into a deep sleep. During this time, the cleaner has no fear of being eaten by its patient.

Sea Partners Fact

Cleaners play an important role on coral reefs. Without them, scientists believe that many of the fish living there would become sick and die.

A small shrimp cleans the inside of a grouper's mouth. The shrimp knows from its partner's body language that the grouper will not try to eat it.

The cleaner may even enter the mouth of the fish it is cleaning. The fish being cleaned could easily eat the cleaner but never does. If you ate your doctor, who would take care of you the next time you were sick?

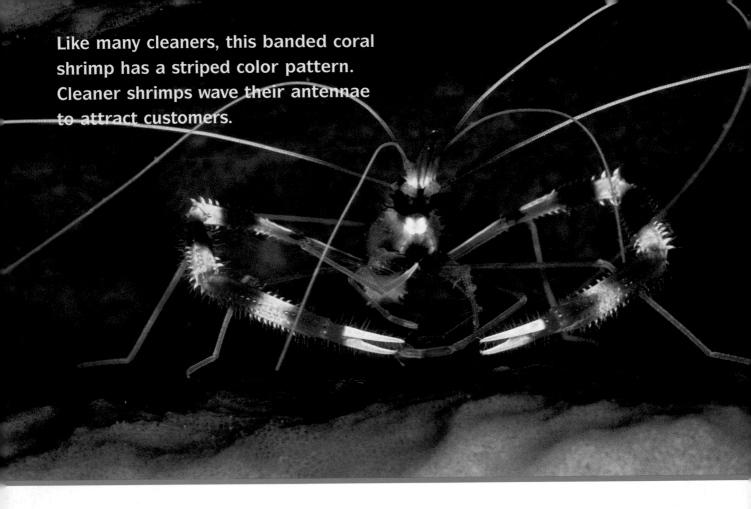

Like many cleaners, this banded coral shrimp has a striped color pattern. Cleaner shrimps wave their antennae to attract customers.

Cleaner Fish and Shrimps

Most cleaners are small fish or shrimps. They often have a striped pattern so that their customers can recognize them. Cleaner shrimps may also be recognized by their long, white antennae, or feelers. When business is slow, cleaner fish may perform a kind of "dance" to attract customers.

This silvertip shark has a small partner. A suckerfish has attached itself to the shark's belly.

A Doctor that Makes House Calls

The remora, or suckerfish, is a hitchhiker. It attaches itself to sharks and other large animals. A special fin on the top of its head works like a suction cup to hold on tightly to its host.

The remora benefits by getting free transportation. It also eats scraps left over from the shark's meals. The shark benefits too, as the remora removes and eats parasites attached to the shark.

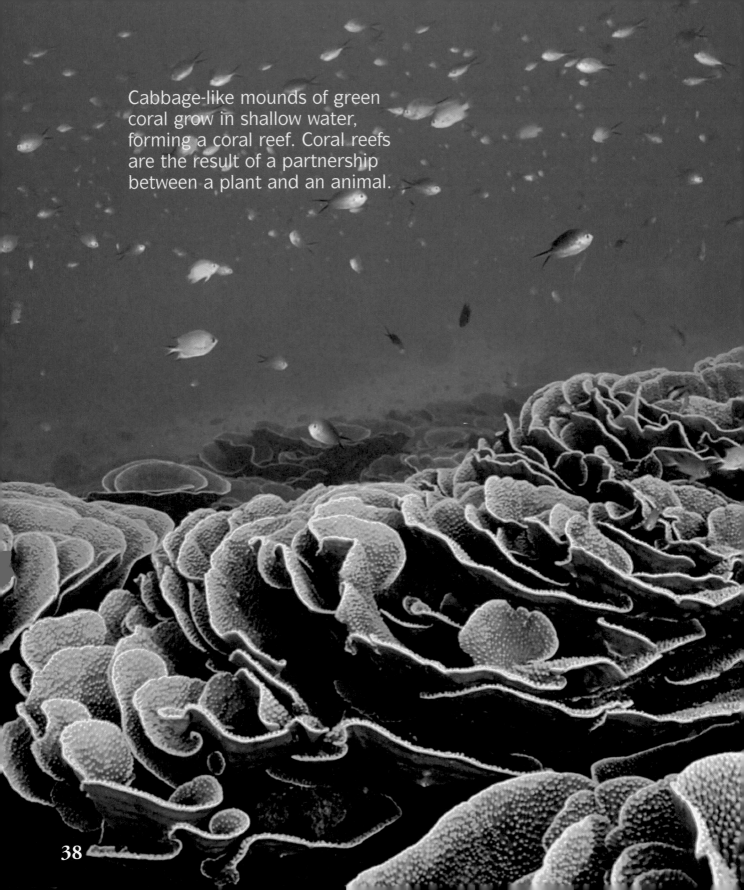

Cabbage-like mounds of green coral grow in shallow water, forming a coral reef. Coral reefs are the result of a partnership between a plant and an animal.

chapter 6

Solar-Powered Animals

Partnerships between plants and animals are among the most important ones in the ocean. Plants use sunlight to make sugar and other foods. Most ocean plants are simple ones called **algae** (AL-jee). Some algae are so small you would need a microscope to see them.

There are millions of tiny algae living inside the bodies of some ocean animals. These algae use sunlight to make food for themselves and for their animal partners. In return, the animals' waste products act like fertilizer does in a garden—they help the plants to grow.

Solar-Powered Corals

Many corals have algae partners inside their bodies. Corals are animals related to sea anemones. Each individual coral animal, called a **coral polyp** (POL-ip), is small. A colony of many coral polyps, however, can be very large.

Reef-building hard corals get their color and most of their food from the tiny plant partners that live inside their bodies.

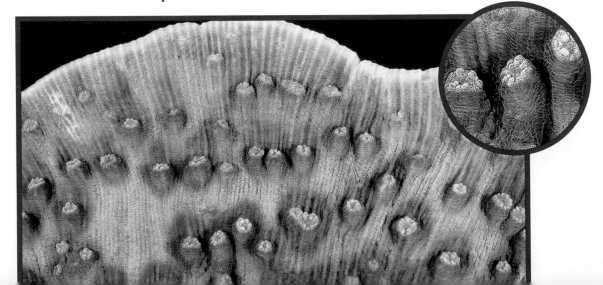

Some corals have a hard limestone skeleton. Over a period of many years, they can create large underwater structures called coral reefs. Coral reefs are found mainly in warm, shallow ocean water, where there is plenty of sunlight. Coral reefs provide homes for more than one-quarter of all known species of ocean animals.

Corals need a lot of food to grow. Most of this food comes from their algae partners. Without this solar-powered partnership, coral reefs would not exist.

Solar-Powered Jellyfish

There are jellyfish that do not sting. Their tentacles do not have stingers for capturing prey. Instead, the algae inside their bodies provides them with all the food they need.

These jellyfish swim toward the sun, because their plant partners need sunlight.

Giant Clams

Giant clams are among the world's largest invertebrate animals. They can be more than 3 feet (1 meter) across and weigh as much as 400 pounds (180 kilograms).

When the clam's shell is open, you can see the animal's colorful flesh inside. This color comes from the plants that live inside the clam's body. No two giant clams have the same color pattern.

Giant clams are filter feeders. However, they also benefit from the extra food supplied by their algae partners.

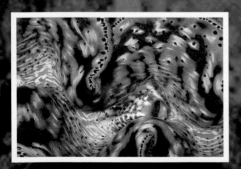  

Giant clams get their color from the tiny plants that live under their skin. No two clams have exactly the same color pattern.

These solar-powered jellyfish live in saltwater lakes near the sea. Each day, the jellyfish swim from one side of the lake to the other. They follow the sun as it moves across the sky. The jellyfish sense that their algae partners produce more food when they receive more sunlight.

More to Learn

We have a great deal to learn about the relationships between living things. This is true both on land and in the sea. We now know that there is a lot more to many relationships than one animal eating another. In fact, many animals and plants live together in permanent relationships with one another. These relationships are usually beneficial to one or both partners.

One thing seems certain. As we continue to study animals that live in the ocean, we will discover more of these fascinating "partnerships in the sea."

Glossary

algae (**AL-jee**) the simplest ocean plants. Some are so small that you would need a microscope to see them. *(pg. 39)*

commensal (**kuh-MEN-sul**) describes a relationship in which one partner benefits and the other is not affected. It is also the name given to the smaller partner who lives with a larger host. *(pg. 8)*

coral polyp (**POL-ip**) an individual coral animal. *(pg. 40)*

coral reef a shallow ocean habitat usually found in warm, tropical water. Coral reefs are built up gradually from the limestone skeletons of small animals called corals. *(pg. 9)*

echinoderm (**ee-KI-no-derm**) a spiny-skinned invertebrate animal. Echinoderms include sea stars, featherstars, and sea urchins. *(pg. 27)*

filter feeding a method of feeding that involves straining seawater with a fine net. Tiny, floating animals and plants are trapped and then eaten. *(pg. 12)*

host an animal that has a smaller symbiotic partner or parasite. *(pg. 7)*

invertebrate (**in-VER-tuh-brate**) an animal without a backbone. Crabs, sea anemones, sea urchins, sponges, and jellyfish are invertebrates. *(pg. 11)*

mutualism (MEW-chew-ul-izm) a relationship in which both partners benefit. *(pg. 6)*

parasite (PAR-uh-site) an animal that lives on or in a host and which causes harm to that host. *(pg. 9)*

predator (PRED-uh-tor) an animal that hunts and kills other animals for food. *(pg. 8)*

prey (PRAY) an animal that is killed and eaten by another animal. *(pg. 25)*

species (SPEE-sees) a particular kind of plant or animal. *(pg. 9)*

symbiosis (SIM-bee-o-sis) a relationship between two different species that benefits one or both. *(pg. 5)*

Learn More About Partners

Books

Cerullo, Mary M. Photographs by Jeffrey L. Rotman. *Coral Reef: A City That Never Sleeps*. Dutton Books, 1996.

Hoff, Mary King. *Living Together*. Creative Education, 2002.

Llamas, Andreu, Gabriel Casadevall, and Ali Garousi. *Sponges: Filters of the Sea*. Gareth Stevens Publishing, 1997.

Silverstein, Alvin, et al. *Symbiosis*. Twenty-First Century Books, 1998.

Web sites

Nemo Facts and Fictions. New England Aquarium, Boston.
(http://neaq2.securesites.net/special/nemo/)

Index

About the Authors

After earning degrees in zoology and medicine, **David Hall** has worked for the past twenty-five years as both a wildlife photojournalist and a physician. David's articles and photographs have appeared in hundreds of calendars, books, and magazines, including *National Geographic, Smithsonian, Natural History,* and *Ranger Rick.* His underwater images have won many major awards including *Nature's Best,* BBC Wildlife Photographer of the Year, and Festival Mondial de l'Image Sous-Marine.

Mary Jo Rhodes received her M.S. in Library Service from Columbia University and was a librarian for the Brooklyn Public Library. She later worked for ten years in children's book publishing in New York City. Mary Jo lives with her husband, John Rounds, and two teenage sons, Jeremy and Tim, in Hoboken, New Jersey.

About the Consultants

Daphne Fautin is a marine biologist. She earned her Ph.D. at the University of California, Berkeley, and she has been a professor of biology at the California Academy of Sciences and the University of Kansas. Daphne is co-author of the book *Anemonefishes and Their Host Sea Anemones.*

Karen Gowlett-Holmes is a marine biologist. She has worked as collection manager of marine invertebrates for the South Australia Museum and for the Australian governmental scientific research organization, CSIRO. Karen is the author of more than 40 scientific papers.